THE HILLS OF LEICESTERSHIRE AND RUTLAND

A guide to walking the hills of Leicestershire and Rutland and places to see when you are there. The hills are defined as summits with a drop of 30 metres (98.4ft) on all sides. In hill walking parlance, these summits are called 'TuMPs' (Thirty upwards Metres Prominence).

There are thirty-two hills in Leicestershire and Rutland that qualify as TuMPs and/or County Tops. For the purposes of this book, they are split into five sections, Charnwood Forest, North Leicestershire, South Leicestershire, East Leicestershire, and Rutland. Eight further hills have been added because of their historical interest or interesting location. This gives forty hills which are arguably the best in Leicestershire and Rutland.

By
Barry K. Smith

'This is a great way to explore Leicestershire and Rutland'

Published by Where2walk

Copyright@2020 Barry K. Smith

The right of Barry K. Smith to be identified as the Author of the work has been asserted by him in accordance with the Copyright, Designs, and Patents Act 1988.

All rights reserved. No part of this publication may be reproduced, stored in a retrieval system or transmitted in any form or by any means, electronic, mechanical, photocopying, recording or otherwise, without the prior permission of the author.

ISBN: 978-0-9956735-3-3

Every reasonable effort has been made by the author to trace copyright holders of material in this book. Any errors or omissions should be notified in writing to the author, who will endeavour to rectify the situation for any future reprints.

Designed and published by Where2walk

SECOND EDITION 2022

Printed by LT Print Group | www.ltprintgroup.co.uk

INDEX

		Page No
1	Introduction	4-7
2	Information on TuMPs	8
3	Access to the hills	9
4	Charnwood Forest	10-19
5	North Leicestershire	20-25
6	South Leicestershire	26-33
7	East Leicestershire	34-43
8	Rutland	44-49
9	Eight more hills not to be missed	50-59
10	Cycling round the hills	60-63
11	My ten favourite hills	64-65
12	Listing by height and map of the hills	66-67
13	Index	68-69

Some hill summits are on private property or on land where there is no public right of way. Permission should be sought from the landowner where access to a hill summit is through private land.

Introduction

Some people refer to it as 'Middle England', others call it the flatlands, but the counties of Leicestershire and Rutland are two of the most beautiful and historical counties in Britain. Leicestershire may be best known for Richard III and the Battle of Bosworth, or its football team winning the Premier League against all odds in 2015/6. However, both it and Rutland have considerably more to offer.

Having lived in Leicestershire for the past 25 years, I thought I should get to know the area better. Much of the best walking and views in any area can be found by visiting its hills, and Leicestershire and Rutland are no exception. I purchased four Ordnance Survey maps (O/S 1:50 Landranger 129, 130, 140 and 141) covering Leicestershire and Rutland. Alternatively, the more detailed O/S 1:25 Explorer maps 232, 233, 234, 245 and 246 could be used.

There are no mountains in Leicestershire and Rutland. A mountain in Britain needs to be 2,000ft high, over 1,000ft higher than Bardon Hill, the highest point in Leicestershire and Rutland. There are hills, however, and the best way of defining these hills is to set a fixed drop between one high point and another. Thirty metres, just under 100ft, is a popular choice of drop and the one I have adopted.

There are 31 hills with this level of drop on all sides in Leicestershire and Rutland. These hills are known as TuMPs (Thirty upwards Metres Prominence) and they are listed on pages 66 and 67. I have added Cold Overton Park Hill (the highest point in Rutland) and eight other hills which should not be missed, 40 hills in total.

The majority of the hills are not difficult to climb, four are in high villages or hamlets so require hardly any walking. There are also a few summits on private land and these should only be visited with permission from the landowner. Where there are access problems that I am aware of, these are raised under the individual hill. Further details on access are included on page 9. This book provides a route to the summit where access is possible.

THE HILLS OF LEICESTERSHIRE AND RUTLAND

I recommend that Ordnance Survey maps are used to supplement the notes in the book. These show paths and rights of way. I have included grid references throughout, including all the summits, so the maps can be used effectively with the notes in this book.

On the walks, you will come across and use footpaths on the 'Leicestershire Round'. This route was devised in 1987 by members of the Leicestershire footpath association as a walk of 100 miles circling Leicestershire.

I have divided the hills into six sections, Charnwood Forest between Leicester and Loughborough, North Leicestershire including the Wolds, South Leicestershire, East Leicestershire, Rutland, and eight hills not to be missed. Further sections have been added on cycling around the hills (many of the hills are close to quiet roads), and my favourite ten hills.

These walks are suitable for all the family, and all ages.

Summit of Ambion Hill.

Introduction (cont)

1. Charnwood Forest (7 hills)

Charnwood Forest is the highest area in Leicestershire and lies north west of Leicester near junction 22 of the M1. Bardon Hill, the highest point in the region, is an interesting climb. It is a unique summit, unlike any other place in Britain, with the quarry falling away to the north, and woodland to the south. The other notable hills in Charnwood Forest include Beacon Hill and Old John Tower in Bradgate Park, probably the two most climbed hills in Leicestershire. All the Charnwood Forest hills have rocky summits.

2. North Leicestershire (4 hills)

The Leicestershire Wolds are in North Leicestershire, rolling countryside mostly over 500ft high. The high points tend to be situated in small villages, inhabited for hundreds of years. This is a good area to cycle round as none of the hills require you to dismount from the bike.

3. South Leicestershire (8 hills)

South of Leicester the hills are scattered. Croft Hill, a few miles south east of Leicester city centre, has been popular since Victorian times. Many walkers and people just out for a picnic, frequent this beautiful spot. An interesting area to explore lies to the south east of Leicester, near Market Harborough. Here you can discover the Langton Caudle and Slawston Hill. The area south and west of Leicester is undulating but lower, never rising above 500ft.

4. East Leicestershire (9 hills)

There are many hills in East Leicestershire, between Melton Mowbray and the A47, Leicester to Uppingham road. These hills are less frequented than those in Charnwood Forest, but there are some surprising places. For example, Burrough Hill, with its Iron Age Fort on the summit, was a popular place to live before Roman times. The highest hill in this area is Whatborough Hill, a HuMP as it has a drop of 100 metres on all sides. Robin-a-Tiptoe Hill, an Iron Age Hill Fort, is prominent, when seen from the surrounding hills.

THE HILLS OF LEICESTERSHIRE AND RUTLAND

View north from near Life Hill, East Leicestershire.

5. Rutland (4 hills)

Rutland is a separate county. It has always been associated with Leicestershire, so I have included it as part of this book. It adds four hills to the list, all interesting in their own way. Hambleton Hill stands on an inlet and overlooks Rutland Water, the largest lake in England with many sporting activities. Prestley Hill will take you to the honey-coloured village of Lyddington. Cold Overton Park Hill is included as it is the County Top.

6. Other hills not to be missed (8 hills)

The final section contains eight other hills which should not be missed. In this second edition, I have added two hills, Timberwood Hill and Launde Park Hill (both give excellent walks) and taken out Bringhurst. This gives a total number of 40 hills and these are listed on pages 66 and 67.

Why bother climbing the hills of Leicestershire and Rutland? The answer is that you will get to know these two historical counties in a unique way, see some fabulous sights and views, and complete some lovely walks.

General Information on TuMPs

A TuMP (Thirty upwards Metres Prominence) is a hill in England, Scotland, or Wales, which is separated from the surrounding landscape by a height difference of at least thirty metres on all sides. At the last count there were over 17,000 TuMPs according to the Relative Hills Society website (rhsoc.uk). This number changes with the finding of new TuMPs and demotions of some TuMPs by bagging enthusiasts. There are high densities of TuMPs in mountainous areas.

In 2013, the TuMPs were added to the database of British and Irish Hills and more information can be found at hill-bagging.co.uk. The Relative Hills Society maintains a record of those who have completed over 2,000 TuMPs and entered the TuMP 'Hall of Fame'. At the end of 2019 eight hill baggers had passed the 5,000 threshold and two were past 8,000. The entries in the hill bagging website for Leicestershire and Rutland can be found by going to 'TuMPs league by County' then clicking on Leicestershire or Rutland.

The War Memorial and Old John in Bradgate Park (a TuMP)

THE HILLS OF LEICESTERSHIRE AND RUTLAND

Countryside Code

Please follow the countryside code. The rules are as follows

1. You should use public rights of way, for example footpaths or bridleways.
2. Use gates, stiles or gaps in field boundaries if you can. Climbing over gates, walls, or fences can damage them.
3. Leave gates as you find them or follow instructions on signs.
4. Leave farm animals alone. Don't interfere with animals if you think they are in distress, try to alert the farmer instead.
5. When you take your dog out, always ensure it does not disturb wildlife, farm animals or other people. Dogs must be kept on a lead at all times when near livestock.
6. Do not block gateways, driveways or other paths with your vehicle.
7. Follow paths unless wider access is available, such as open country or registered common land.
8. When driving, slow down or stop for horses, walkers and farm animals, and give them plenty of room.

Rules on Access

Access to these hills may be over private land. This is fine if accessed via a footpath or with permission of the landowner. It is only possible to climb a few of these hills if prior permission has been sought and granted from the landowners. I have mentioned these hills in the text.

If a sign is encountered denying access, then please do not ignore this.

The existence of this list is not an encouragement to break the law, interfere with landowners' privacy or trespass on land to which there is no legal access.

Area Introduction

1. CHARNWOOD FOREST

Charnwood Forest is the highest land in Leicestershire and Rutland, most of the 'Forest' is higher than 600ft (180m). It lies in north west Leicestershire bounded by Leicester, Loughborough and Coalville. The area is undulating, rocky at the highest points, and picturesque with extensive areas of woodland. On its west side lies an abandoned coalfield now being regenerated and replanted as part of the National Forest. The M1 motorway, between junctions 21 and 23, cuts through the middle of Charnwood Forest.

Seven of the Leicestershire hills (TuMPs) lie in Charnwood Forest. They are listed below;

	Height	Prominence	Page No
Bardon Hill	280m / 918 ft	172m	12
Birch Hill	254m / 833 ft	31m	13
Beacon Hill	248m / 814 ft	62m	14
Benscliffe Hill	237m / 778 ft	39m	15
Bawdon Castle	232m / 761 ft	34m	16
Old John Tower	212m / 696 ft	35m	17
Ives Head	201m / 659 ft	43m	19

Opposite, on the way up Bardon Hill.

Bardon Hill (280m, 918ft)

O/S Landranger 129, Summit Ref SK 460132

Bardon Hill is the highest point in Leicestershire and the National Forest. It is well known in hill bagging circles because it is one of the most 'remote' Marilyns (hills in Britain with a 150m drop on all sides) being about 50 miles from its nearest neighbour. It is also a surprising hill. Bardon Hill is a former volcano and now has two faces, the east side having been removed by Bardon Hill quarry and the west side preserved as a site of scientific interest.

The Bardon Hill quarry produces about three million tonnes of crushed rock per year, which is around 15% of the normal year's production for the whole of the UK. The rock is used to build roads and for the foundation of buildings. The west side of Bardon Hill is a Site of Special Scientific Interest because it has veins of quartz containing copper and gold. In addition, the volcanic rocks have been eroded to form 'wadis' and these have been infilled by red coloured desert sediments.

The usual route of ascent starts at Vercor Close on the north side of the hill. Vercor Close is one kilometre north of the summit (grid ref SK 458141). This route avoids the quarry. Vercor Close is in a housing estate a short distance from the A50 Coalville bypass. From here a public footpath leads south towards the summit. The summit is just east of the radio mast which can be seen from the road.

From Vercor Close follow the public footpath south for 300m to a wood. Turn left along the right of way. After 100m, turn right to follow a good track up the hill. Go past a stone bench and through a kissing gate. Follow the path to the transmitter. There is a path which goes west towards the edge of the quarry. After 100m the Trig Point appears, perched on a built-up rock overlooking a large quarry.

At the summit of Bardon Hill.

Birch Hill (254m, 833ft)

O/S Landranger 129, Summit Ref SK 478136

Birch Hill lies just west of the M1 near junction 2. It is the second highest hill in Leicestershire and there are good views north from near the summit. The extra height of this part of Charnwood Forest creates 360-degree views.

The highest point is in woodland which is completely surrounded by an ancient stone wall. This has been damaged by people climbing over it, so access to the summit, which is on private land, is not permitted. A right of way starting at grid ref SK 480131 runs close to the summit and walkers must stop when reaching the wall (this is only a few metres below the height of the summit). The highest point is on rocks by a wind turbine cable. This can be seen from outside the wood.

Beacon Hill (248m, 814ft)

O/S Landranger 129, Summit Ref SK 510148

Beacon Hill is often thought to be the highest point in Leicestershire because of its magnificent summit area and the feeling that this is a 'proper hill'. It lies close to Loughborough so it is a hill I have climbed many times. After I had lived in Leicestershire for some years, I found that the Bardon Hill is higher.

Beacon Hill was the site of a Bronze Age Hill Fort. Today a view finder indicates places that can be seen on a clear day. These include Lincoln Cathedral and the Peak District.

Looking north east from the view finder on Beacon Hill.

Beacon Hill lies in its own Country Park and has two car parks for visitors. The lower one is to be found just off the road from Nanpantan to Woodhouse Eves, opposite Charnwood Golf Club (grid ref SK 522148). The higher one lies off the B591 just over a mile west of Woodhouse Eves.

It is a very short walk north to the summit from the higher car park. The Trig Point can be seen from the car park.

I prefer to ascend the hill from the lower car park, a return walk of two miles on good paths. It is shorter to take the southerly path out of the car park but both paths lead to the summit. The summit is a joy with a Trig Point and a View Finder. The Trig Point is higher.

Benscliffe Hill (237m, 778ft)

O/S Landranger 129, Summit Ref SK 513127

Benscliffe Hill lies midway between Beacon Hill and Old John Tower. Benscliffe Hill is on private land so there is no access without permission. As with all the Charnwood Forest hills there are good views to the east and Leicester.

Benscliffe Wood, in which the hill is situated, is a site of special scientific interest. The wood has one of the richest varieties of lichens in the East Midlands, with over 30 species growing on Precambrian rocks.

There is a log gate on the west side of the road from Shepshed to Newton Linford with a sign confirming no public access (grid ref SK 517128). This signifies the eastern side of the 24 acres of woodland. The summit lies about four hundred metres to the west of the log gate. Like all the Charnwood Forest hills, the highest areas are rocky. in this case the summit is a big rock amidst brambles.

Bawdon Castle (232m, 761ft)

O/S Landranger 129, Summit Ref SK 495143

Start of the walk up Bawdon Castle.

Bawdon Castle is the lowest of the five summits, all with names beginning with B, that lie in the central area of Charnwood Forest. A right of way passes close to the summit.

There are good views over Beacon Hill and it is possible to combine this summit with Beacon Hill. There are two alternative start points, from the minor road between Woodhouse Eves and Copt Oak (grid ref SK 495138), or from the minor road just to the east (grid ref SK 497149). It is easier to park on the minor road to the east so I recommend this route if you are driving. Both routes follow a path until 100m from the summit.

From the minor road to the east, you should head west. Follow the right of way signs round a wooded area to join the path from the B5350. Walk south east along this path until you are 100m east of the summit. You will find a path which leads to a radio mast. This is where you should stop unless you have permission, because it is a no through route on private land. The summit, which is 50m west of the radio mast, is a large rocky tor.

Old John Tower (212m, 696ft)

O/S Landranger 129, Summit Ref SK 525112

Driving down London Road towards Leicester Railway Station on a fine day, Bradgate Park can be seen directly ahead. Old John, sometimes known as 'The Jug' is one of the best-known sites in Leicestershire. The highest point, by a small margin, is 150m to the west, just north of the War Memorial.

Old John was built as a ruined folly in 1784, and adapted in the 19th Century to serve as an observation tower for the practice circuit, laid out by the seventh Earl Grey for his horses. Internally the tower retains a number of 19th century fittings including timber floors, slate fireplaces, shuttered windows and a castellated roof. The tower is a grade two listed building and is open to visitors on the park's guided walk programmes.

Bradgate Park passed into the Grey Family in 1445 when Edward married William de Ferrers' only surviving daughter. It remained in the Grey family for 500 years. Lady Jane Grey, who was de facto Queen of England and Ireland for nine days in 1553, was born at Bradgate House (now in ruins) in 1537.

Today the park is owned by the Bradgate Park Charitable Trust. The landscape is rocky moorland covered in coarse grass and bracken. There are several areas of woodland enclosed by stone walls that are not accessible to the Public, and the park is home to herds of red deer and fallow deer. However, the vast majority of the park is open to the public.

CHARNWOOD FOREST

Old John Tower (cont)

The Hunts Hill car park just north of Old John Tower gives an easy walk to Old John and the War Memorial which lies about 150m to the west of Old John. The highest point is approximately 50m north of the War Memorial.

A proper perspective of Bradgate Park can be obtained by walking to the Memorial and Old John Tower from the car park at the Hallgate Entrance (grid ref SK 542114). It is possible to visit the café and Visitors Centre, see the red deer, and enjoy a walk over rocky moorland past ancient buildings.

From the car park, walk nearly one mile south on a good path. This will take you to the café and Visitors Centre. From there walk 1.5 miles north west, on good paths, to the summit of the Memorial, then Old John. The return route takes a direct route east back to the car park going over point 178m.

Old John.

Ives Head (201m, 659ft)

O/S Landranger 129, Summit Ref SK 478170

Ives Head is an attractive hill close to Shepshed. There are good views east over Loughborough. The area is a geological site of special scientific interest as it exposes volcaniclastic sandstones dating back 600 million years.

If cycling to the hill or walking from Shepshed, there is a stile on the left side of the road. The stile is just south of the high point on the minor road, which runs along the west side of the hill (grid ref SK 472174). After climbing over the stile, there is a grassy path which leads to the summit of the hill.

There is a parking area at the crossroads west of the summit (grid ref SK 472169). From here walk north up the road to Shepshed (there is a path on the left side of the road) to the stile, then follow the grassy path south east to the summit, a rocky outcrop with a dominating Trig Point.

Ives Head, summit back left, in late evening sunshine.

Area Information

2. North Leicestershire

North Leicestershire is defined as anywhere north of Loughborough and Melton Mowbray. The common feature of the four 'summits' in this area is that you don't have to walk far from the car to reach the high point.

Three of the four summits are on the Leicestershire Wolds. The Wolds form a watershed between the rivers Wreake, Soar and Trent with streams draining from the central elevated land to these rivers. Two of the three summits are situated in villages, Waltham on the Wolds and Buckminster, with the third, Broughton Hill, situated in a hamlet accessed through an avenue of trees.

The fourth summit in North Leicestershire is Breedon Hill which lies in the far north west corner of Leicestershire, close to the border with Derbyshire. It is near East Midlands Airport and the Donington Motor Racing Circuit.

The hills are listed below;

	Height	Prominence	Page No
Waltham on the Wolds Hill	177m / 581 ft	66m	22
Broughton Hill	173m / 568 ft	37m	23
Buckminster Hill	158m / 518 ft	35m	24
Breedon Hill	126m / 414 ft	30m	25

Opposite, isolated church of St Mary and St Hardolph on Breedon Hill.

NORTH LEICESTERSHIRE

Waltham on the Wolds Hill (177m, 581ft)

O/S Landranger map 130, Summit Ref SK 806245

Waltham on the Wolds is a quiet village on the A607, on the road from Melton Mowbray to Grantham, in the far north east of Leicestershire. It has a church, a pub and a village hall. The village lies on the Leicestershire Wolds. There is an escarpment north of Waltham on the Wolds overlooking the Vale of Belvoir and Belvoir Castle (see page 53).

It is difficult to identify the highest point. I suggest parking anywhere in Waltham on the Wolds and walking to the reservoir, near the Water Tower, see picture below. The grassy hill surrounding the reservoir looks higher than any other point in the village but, being man made, it does not qualify. The high point may be somewhere in the farm to the west of the reservoir, but it is very marginal. For the purposes of this list, the highest point is deemed to be on the road next to the reservoir.

Waltham on the Wolds Hill, farm and reservoir.

THE HILLS OF LEICESTERSHIRE AND RUTLAND

Broughton Hill (173m, 568ft)

O/S Landranger map 129, Summit Ref SK 712239

Broughton Hill lies just north of Melton Mowbray and is the highest point of an area of elevated ground which falls off rapidly to the north, less so to the south. The high point is only 300m to the west of the A606 as it runs south east from Nottingham to Melton Mowbray. Driving from Nottingham, the A606 passes Nether Broughton, then rises 80m to 171m (only two metres lower than the summit) at the crossroads with the B676, near Broughton Hill.

On one 'ascent' I cycled east along the former Roman road from Six Hills (B676). The road rises gradually as it follows the northern ridge of the Wolds, with views appearing to the north. A few hundred metres before the crossroads with the A606, a lane goes off to the left. It is best to walk or cycle 200m up this lane to a crossroads. If driving, it is possible to park just off the B676 and walk up the lane. The highest point is unmarked but obvious, ten metres north of the crossroads.

Avenue of trees and flowers at the summit of Broughton Hill.

NORTH LEICESTERSHIRE

Buckminster Hill (158m, 518ft)

O/S Landranger 130, Summit Ref SK 880229

The two village hills of Waltham on the Wolds (page 22) and Buckminster both lie east of Melton Mowbray and are usually combined, either by car or by bike. The summit of Buckminster Hill lies in the village of Buckminster, ten miles east of Melton Mowbray, close to the Lincolnshire border.

Buckminster Park stands at the north east end of the village. Buckminster Hall was built in the park in the 1790s by Sir William Manners, rebuilt in the 1960s. The St John the Baptist church was built between 1250 and 1350 and is richly decorated with carvings.

The high point is on School Lane, off the crossroads to the east of the village, but it is worth having a walk round this pretty village, and maybe a visit to the pub. There is no higher ground from here to the east coast of England.

Cricket ground at Buckminster close to the high point.

Breedon Hill (127m, 417ft)

O/S Landranger 129, Summit Ref SK 405233

Twenty miles west of the other three hills in North Leicestershire lies the isolated but spectacular village of Breedon on the Hill. The summit of Breedon Hill stands above the village. The area used to be an Iron Age hill fort occupied between the first Century BC and first Century AD. A recent survey indicated that the drop is only 29.8m, just under the 30m required for a TuMP. The difference is small so I have left the hill on this list.

The isolated church of St Mary and St Hardulph now stands on the site of the Iron Age Fort and a former Augustinian priory (picture, page 21). The church contains one of England's largest collections of Saxon carvings including the Breedon Angel, considered to be the earliest carved Angel in England.

The high point is at the back of the graveyard to the west of the church. I recommend the walk to the top from the village, a fine walk in the sunshine.

Breedon Hill from the east.

Area Information

3. South Leicestershire

South Leicestershire covers the hills in Leicestershire south of the A47 as it runs east from Leicester to Peterborough, and the hills south of the A511 as it runs west from Leicester to Burton on Trent. The main towns are Hinckley, Lutterworth and Market Harborough. It is an area rich in history, now mainly devoted to farming.

Two of the hills lie in the west of the region towards the border with Warwickshire. This gives the opportunity for an excellent day out with visits to Bosworth Battlefield (see page 52) and Twycross Zoo. Four of the remaining six hills are between Market Harborough and the A47.

The hills are listed below;

	Height	**Prominence**	**Page No**
Bassett's Hill	182m / 596 ft	33m	28
Mowsley Hills	177m / 581 ft	35m	29
Moor Hill	172m / 565 ft	34m	28
Langton Caudle	147m / 482 ft	50m	30
South Hill	132m / 433 ft	39m	33
Slawston Hill	131m / 430 ft	37m	31
Croft Hill	128m / 420 ft	44m	32
Wellsborough Hill	120m / 394 ft	31m	33

Opposite, walking up the Langton Caudle.

THE HILLS OF LEICESTERSHIRE AND RUTLAND

SOUTH LEICESTERSHIRE

Bassett's Hill (182m, 596ft)

O/S Landranger 141, Summit Ref SP 766987

Moor Hill (172m, 565ft)

O/S Landranger 141, Summit Ref SP 781987

Bassett's Hill and Moor Hill lie south of Tugby, a village just off the A47, Leicester to Uppingham road. They are only 1.5km apart so both hills can be completed together. Tugby and Keythorpe are home to nine listed buildings including the church of St Thomas Beckett.

It is difficult to combine the two hills in a single walk as there is no Right of Way which leads to Moor Hill from Bassett's Hill. Unfortunately, this has meant that Moor Hill is effectively a 'drive-by hill'. It will be noted that Ram's Head Spinney is the highest point in this area, climbed by a short walk from its east side, but it is not a TuMP and therefore not included in this book.

Large pond near Keythorpe Hall Farm.

THE HILLS OF LEICESTERSHIRE AND RUTLAND

To climb Bassett's Hill, park at the crossroads 400m north of Keythorpe Hall Farm (grid ref SP 765999). Walk south for nearly one mile passing Keythorpe Hall Farm, and then climb 100ft to reach the top of Bassett's Hill. There is a Trig Point in the hedge, but it is difficult to find. The summit of Moor Hill is on East Norton to Hallaton road, just south of Moor Hill Farm. By selecting the high point of the road around this point, you will be able to 'tick' the summit.

Mowsley Hills (177m, 581ft)

O/S Landranger 140, Summit Ref SP 633885

Anyone leaving the centre of Leicester and heading south on the Welford Road, will pass the home of Leicester Tigers (Leicester's famous rugby team). Continuing south the road passes through Wigston, then the ground rises to the village of Mowsley. Turn right just before a large wind turbine. After 300m, a track appears on the right and there is space to park. Walk north up the mast track for 300m to the Reservoir compound where the Trig Point is located. This is the most southerly summit in Leicestershire.

Trig Point at the summit of Mowsley Hills.

SOUTH LEICESTERSHIRE

Langton Caudle (147m, 482ft)

O/S Landranger 141, Summit Ref SP 745942

The Langtons, which include the villages of Tur Langton, Church Langton, East and West Langton, and Thorpe Langton, lie a few miles north of Market Harborough in a beautiful part of Leicestershire. The Langton Caudle, a gracious hill with good paths up it, overlooks the villages. To appreciate this part of South East Leicestershire, I suggest a walk of six miles starting at Tur Langton. Walk east to Stonton Wyville, south over the Langton Caudle to Thorpe Langton, and then back to Tur Langton.

Summit of the Langton Caudle.

The shortest route up the Langton Caudle, however, is from the north west. There is room to park on the rough road running south (grid ref SP 737947). A good path, part of the Leicestershire Round, leads to the summit. It is 2km up and down.

THE HILLS OF LEICESTERSHIRE AND RUTLAND

Slawston Hill (131m, 430ft)

O/S Landranger 141, Summit Ref SP 783941

Slawston Hill stands on a grassy hill with patches of gorse, just to the south east of the village of Slawston, north of Market Harborough. There is a Trig Point and good views from the summit. Nearby lies Slawston Bridge, a former railway bridge, which is popular with rock climbers. On a recent visit I found six climbers enjoying the sunshine and completing rock climbs on the railway bridge.

Summit of Slawston Hill.

The hill lies close to the Slawston to Medbourne road. As you pass to the south west of the hill, there is a gate on the north side of the road (grid ref SP 782940). There is parking on the gravel road to the south east of the hill and it is then possible to visit the railway bridge and walk to the gate.

Permission should be obtained to climb to the Trig Point of Slawston Hill. The summit is about 150m north west of the gate at the top the hill. The highest point is a grassy knoll 50m north east of the Trig Point.

SOUTH LEICESTERSHIRE

Croft Hill (128m, 420ft)

O/S Landranger 141, Summit Ref SP 510967

Croft Hill stands 128m high, rising up on the Soar flood-plain just south of Leicester. It is a distinct hill that can be seen from many miles away.

Summit of Croft Hill with Croft Quarry behind.

If driving to Croft Hill from Leicester, take the B4114 to Narborough, turn right on a minor road and continue through Huncote. Between Huncote and Croft, next to a post box, there is room for 2/3 cars to park (grid ref SP 509969). Cross the road, go through a gap in the hedge and turn slightly right to follow one of a variety of paths to the summit, a walk of about 200m.

To the east of Croft Hill, the New Hill has been constructed out of quarry waste and has been landscaped and planted. Between the two hills lies an enormous quarry, Croft Quarry. Blasting may be taking place at 1pm during the week and Croft Hill is best avoided at that time.

South Hill (132m, 433ft)

O/S Landranger 140, Summit Ref SK 300081

Both South Hill and Wellsborough Hill lie west of Leicester, the highest points of relatively flat lands. South Hill is the most westerly hill in Leicestershire and is on the border with Warwickshire. To find the hill, leave the M42 at junction 11, drive down the A444 to Appleby Parva and then turn right towards Austrey. Park near the radio mast (grid ref SK 303080).

From here walk along the track 300m north west. The highest point is in the field just to the south. The track also denotes the boundary between Leicestershire and Warwickshire and it is debatable whether this hill is in Leicestershire or Warwickshire.

There are a number of 'additions' that can be made to this walk. One option is to continue on the track and cross the bridge over the M42. A circular walk can then be completed via No Man's Heath and Austrey. Another option is to visit the land next to the water tower (grid ref SK 304076), not far from the radio mast. This is a similar height to the summit.

Wellsborough Hill (120m, 394ft)

O/S Landranger 140, Summit Ref SK 364024

It is seven miles from South Hill to Wellsborough Hill, one of the lowest hills on the list at only 120 metres (394ft) above sea level. Despite the lack of height, the view to the south east stretches over many miles of countryside.

Wellsborough is a small village two miles east of Market Bosworth. Bosworth Battlefield is two miles south of Market Bosworth (see page 52).

It is a short walk to the high point from the centre of Wellsborough. There is parking opposite the school in a pull off area. The highest point is 100m south of the gate, near the corner of the hedge next to a large mast. The ground falls away to give a good view east. Croft Hill can be seen in the distance.

Area Information

4. East Leicestershire

East Leicestershire covers the area bounded by the A607 from Leicester to Melton Mowbray, to the north, and the A47 from Leicester to Peterborough road, to the south. This area contains the highest land in Leicestershire outside Charnwood Forest and some of its most interesting hills including Burrough Hill and the group of five hills near Launde Abbey. The area also contains Whatborough Hill, a HuMP (hundred metres or more prominence). The only other HuMP in Leicestershire is Bardon Hill.

The hills are listed below;

	Height	Prominence	Page No
Whatborough Hill	230m / 755 ft	108m	36
Life Hill	226m / 741 ft	46m	39
Robin-a-Tiptoe Hill	222m / 728 ft	43m	37
Colborough Hill	220m / 722 ft	36m	38
Cold Overton Hill	211m / 692 ft	44m	39
Burrough Hill	210m / 689 ft	31m	40
Launde Hill	202m / 663 ft	39m	41
Round Hill	193m / 633 ft	31m	42
Gartree Hill	148m / 486 ft	36m	43

Opposite, Whatborough Hill from its near neighbour, Colborough Hill.

THE HILLS OF LEICESTERSHIRE AND RUTLAND

EAST LEICESTERSHIRE

Whatborough Hill (230m, 755ft)

O/S Landranger 141, Summit Ref SK 767059

Whatborough Hill is a HuMP because it has over a hundred metre drop (prominence) on all sides. It is the highest hill between Charnwood Forest and the Wash. Whatborough used to be a Roman Settlement but was cleared for sheep farming in 1495.

It is straightforward to walk up Whatborough Hill from the south. From the A47 road from Leicester to Peterborough, take the B6047 to Tilton on the Hill, then a road goes west towards Oakham. Follow this for one and a half miles to reach the bottom of the Reservoir access road next to the summit (grid ref SK 766056). There is room to park near the junction on the south side of the road. Walk north up the mast road to the reservoir, then a left turn through a gap in the fence and you will see the Trig Point, which is in the middle of a field, see below.

Summit of Whatborough Hill looking east.

Robin-a-Tiptoe Hill (222m, 728ft)

O/S Landranger 141, Summit Ref SK 774043

Robin-a-Tiptoe Hill lies at the centre of the East Leicestershire 'five hills' and, despite not being the highest summit, it is the dominant hill in the area. Its summit dome can be seen from many places in this part of Leicestershire.

Robin-a-Tiptoe Hill is an impressive hill. Its summit is an old hill fort thought to be used by the Romans. The name, Robin-a-Tiptoe, is said to refer to a sheep rustler who escaped death by hanging, by being unusually tall so his feet touched the ground. It is also the name of a local ale.

If you wish to visit the summit, permission should be requested from the landowners. Since there are sheep grazing on the summit area, dogs are not allowed. There is a right of way which starts north east of the summit and runs south across the side of the hill but it does not cross the highest point.

Robin-a-Tiptoe hill from the north west.

EAST LEICESTERSHIRE

Colborough Hill (220m, 722ft)

O/S Landranger 141, Grid Reference SK 761051

Colborough Hill is a great little hill. I would be happy to walk up it one hundred times if I lived closer. It lies south west of Whatborough Hill and north west of Robin-a-Tiptoe Hill. Next to it lies Tilton Cutting, an old railway line closed in 1965. The Cutting is now a geological site supporting a wide range of wildlife.

A footpath leaves the road from Tilton to Oakham (grid ref SK 761057). There is room to park next to the entrance to Tilton Cutting. Walk south through a gate and follow the path to another gate. You will see the hill rising in front of you across a grassy field, usually with sheep grazing. Follow the path round the right-hand side of the field and then climb to the summit, which is just in front of the trees. The walk up and down the hill is one mile and takes about 30 minutes, perfect before dinner on a summer evening.

Walking up Colborough Hill, the summit is just in front of the trees.

# THE HILLS OF LEICESTERSHIRE AND RUTLAND

Life Hill (226m, 741ft)
O/S Landranger 141, Summit Ref SK 722050

Life Hill lies two kilometres to the west of Tilton on the Hill and is only seven metres higher than the village. Tilton on the Hill is one of the highest places in Leicestershire at over 700ft. It was founded in Saxon times at the crossroads of ancient paths between Leicester, Oakham, Market Harborough and Melton Mowbray. The centre of the village is now a conservation area.

The radio mast close to the summit of Life Hill can be seen from many miles around so the hill is easy to find. It is possible to park near the radio mast. Walk west back along the road to a gate on the south side of the road. The highest point is in the field. A few hundred metres east down the road, there are great views to the north (see picture on page 7).

Cold Overton Hill (211m, 692ft)
O/S Landranger 141, Summit Ref SK 805096

Cold Overton Hill lies just south of the village of Cold Overton, close to the border with Rutland. It can be combined with Ranksborough Hill and Cold Overton Park Hill in Rutland (see pages 46 and 49). Cold Overton village was listed in the Doomsday book and has a long history. It has two Grade 1 listed buildings, the St John the Baptist church with its notable early English carvings, and Cold Overton Hall built in 1664.

The hill is next to the road which runs south from Cold Overton to Knossington. It is possible to park on the side of the road or park in Cold Overton village and walk to a gate (grid ref SK 806097). The summit is at the high point of the field to the south of the gate.

There is an out of use Royal Observer Corps monitoring post just inside the field. These were constructed for the Corps' Nuclear reporting role and operated by volunteers during the cold war, 1955 to 1991.

Burrough Hill (210m, 689ft)

O/S Landranger 129, Summit Ref SK 761118

Burrough Hill stands tall a few miles south of Melton Mowbray. In the Spring, yellow gorse covers the north side of the hill making it clearly visible from miles away. However, it is the summit which is surprising. A large Iron Age Fort of old fortifications, now grassed over, encloses a substantial grassy field which used to be inhabited. The Trig Point, which is the highest point, stands on the east side (picture, page 65). There is a view finder on the west side.

The hill fort dates from the late Bronze or Early Iron Age. Artefacts excavated in recent years indicate that there was intensive activity between 100BC and 50AD and that the settlement had a wide range of trade links. The site was probably in use during the Roman occupation. Later, in medieval times, the locals used the area to hold a fair, as well as for dancing and games.

Spring gorse on Burrough Hill.

Burrough Hill now lies in a Country Park with a car park (charge) to the south east of the hill. This gives an easy walk to the Trig Point and round the old Iron Age Fort. The hill can also be ascended from the north or the west. A footpath ascends from the north giving a pleasant climb to the summit Trig Point. From the west follow the 'Leicestershire Round' path.

Launde Hill (202m, 663ft)

O/S Landranger 141, Summit Ref SK 786042

Launde Hill is the most easterly of the five closely packed hills in the centre of this region. It lies close to Launde Park and Abbey, a Christian Retreat House. The Abbey grounds and tearoom can be visited, check opening times. Park at the Oxey Farm Crossroads (grid ref SK 778034) and walk south east along the road for 500m. There is a right of way which goes north then east to the entrance of Launde Big Wood. This is an ancient wood and nature reserve of 102 acres open to visitors. There are good paths through the wood. The summit is just outside the wood on the north side.

Launde Big Wood.

EAST LEICESTERSHIRE

Round Hill (193m, 633ft)

O/S Landranger 141, Summit Ref SK779029

Round Hill is the lowest of the five hills between Tilton and Tugby. A narrow, winding and hilly road leads north from Tugby. After 2.5km it reaches its high point at a gate close to the summit of Round Hill. There is no parking next to the gate but parking is possible 500m further north at Oxey Farm crossroads, as for Launde Hill (see page 41).

The summit of Round Hill lies just behind the trees.

Walk back to the gate and the summit is about 200m west behind a small wood.

Running between all five of these East Leicestershire hills is the dismantled railway from Nottingham to Market Harborough. Round Hill and Colborough Hill lie just west of the old railway line. Whatborough Hill, Robin-a-Tiptoe Hill and Launde Hill lie just east of the old line.

Gartree Hill (148m, 486ft)

O/S Landranger 129, Summit Ref SK758145

Gartree Hill is an unassuming hill between Burrough Hill and Melton Mowbray. It is easy to ascend by parking just to the south of the hill and walking up the tarmac track. On reaching the highest point of the track, you are faced with twin summits in grassy fields, a few metres to the east and the west of the track. It is thought that the grassy field to the west is marginally higher but there is very little to choose between them.

Cycling up Gartree Hill.

Area Information

5. Rutland

Rutland is the smallest historic County in England and has only two towns, Oakham, the County Town, and Uppingham. It was once royal hunting country. During the reign of William 1, it was designated a forest and preserved for the chasing of deer and wild boar. Little of the forest remains and it is now a mainly agricultural area.

From 1974 until 1997, Rutland was part of Leicestershire but is now, once again, an independent county. It has a population of only 40,000, compared to over 700,000 in Leicestershire.

Rutland is home to the UK's largest man-made lake, Rutland Water. There are many activities centred on Rutland Water. The activities include bikes for hire, which allow you to do a full circuit of the lake, a sailing club, and plenty of walking. Rutland Water even has its own parkrun, with each kilometre marked out along the shoreline.

Rutland's four hills are;

	Height	Prominence	Page No
Ranksborough Hill	191m / 627 ft	41m	46
Hambleton Hill	126m / 413 ft	40m	47
Prestley Hill	117m / 384 ft	38m	48
Cold Overton Park	197m / 646 ft	10m	49

Ranksborough Hill is not the highest point in Rutland. The highest point is a Trig Point to the east of Cold Overton Park Wood at 197m (646ft). This hill does not qualify as a TuMP as it is a subsidiary hill of Cold Overton Hill in Leicestershire. However, as it is a County Top, I have included it as one of the forty hills in this book. Further information is on page 49.

Opposite, Rutland Water and Normanton church.

THE HILLS OF LEICESTERSHIRE AND RUTLAND

RUTLAND

Ranksborough Hill (191m, 627ft)

O/S Landranger 130, Summit Ref SK 822114

Ranksborough Hill is the highest separate hill in Rutland. There is a right of way leading up from the north west, starting just south of Northfield Farm (grid ref SK 813119) and a right of way from Langham to the east. I would recommend the route from Langham, particularly as the village has two pubs for refreshments after the walk.

It is usually possible to park at Ranksborough Hall. The route from there goes through a pleasant holiday park. Follow the right of way from the holiday park and then past a farm. From the farm the path heads north west straight towards the top of Ranksborough Hill. However, there is a ploughed field and it may be necessary to walk round the edge of this field.

From the summit the right of way continues north west reaching the minor road south of Northfield Farm. The hill can also be ascended from there.

Looking towards Langham from near the summit of Ranksborough Hill.

Hambleton Hill (126m, 413ft)

O/S Landranger 141, Summit Ref SK 900076

Hambleton Hill lies in the centre of Upper Hambleton, which is on a peninsula overlooking Rutland Water. The parish originally included the settlements of Upper Hambleton, Middle Hambleton and Nether Hambleton, but the latter two were almost completely submerged by the construction of Rutland Water in 1976. Upper Hambleton is now an attractive village with Hambleton Hall, a hotel and restaurant, and a pub called the Finch's Arms.

The summit is in the church grounds of the 12th century St Andrews church, but a quick visit to the village of Upper Hambleton and its church does not do justice to this picturesque area.

I suggest taking the track from Hambleton Village round the peninsula, a distance of about 7km. This has great views of the lake and its wildlife, and could be followed by a visit to the local pub.

Rutland Water from Hambleton village.

RUTLAND

Prestley Hill (117m, 384ft)

O/S Landranger 141, Summit Ref SP 882973

Prestley Hill is climbed from the attractive Rutland village of Lyddington. Lyddington is a village which should be visited for its Bede House and two pubs with restaurants. The Bede House at Lyddington is a honey-coloured stone building which originated as the medieval wing of a palace belonging to the Bishops of Lincoln. It is open to the public.

The best route up Prestley Hill starts from the road about 300m north of the Bede House (grid ref SP 874973). Follow the road then a track north east for 500m. After 500m the wood on the right ends and fields appear. Turn right and follow the edge of the wood, south east, then east, then south east again as the ground rises to a hedge. This is the highest point that can be reached on a path. The summit is 100m to the west on private land.

Bede House at Lyddington.

Cold Overton Park Hill (197m, 646ft)

O/S Landranger 141, Summit Ref SK 827085

The highest point in the county of Rutland is the Trig Point at the top of Cold Overton Park Hill. This is not a TuMP as it does not have a drop of 30 metres or more on all sides, so does not qualify as one of the thirty-one hills listed on pages 66. The ground only drops about 10 metres (33ft) between this point and Cold Overton Hill, nearly two miles away to the north west and in Leicestershire. However, for completeness and some great views over Rutland Water, I suggest walking to this hill.

Park just off the road from Knossington to Oakham (grid ref SK 830089). From here follow the right of way south, initially on a track then on a path. A field is passed, normally with sheep in it, on your right. After walking about 400m, the path starts a gradual descent. Continue to a gate on the right. The Trig Point is 150m north west of the gate.

The summit of Cold Overton Park Hill, the County Top of Rutland.

Eight other hills not to be missed

The eight hills below have just under 30 metres of prominence, so they do not qualify for the main list. The first two hills have historical significance, in particular Ambion Hill which was where Richard III camped before the Battle of Bosworth in 1485. The third and fourth hill (Launde Park Hill and Smith Hill) combine to give an excellent round from Launde Abbey.

The fifth, sixth and seventh hills are in Charnwood Forest, the first two hills, High Cademan and Knoll Hill, are short walks from the road but have great summits with Trig Points. The third hill, Timberwood Hill, has been added in this second edition. It is a lovely walk to a quiet, but high summit and good views.

The final hill is smaller. Hoton Hills lies on the coast-to-coast route near my home in Loughborough.

The eight hills are:

	Height	Page No
Ambion Hill	120m / 394 ft	52
Belvoir Castle	138m / 453 ft	53
Launde Park Hill	191m / 627 ft	54
Smith Hill	172m / 564 ft	54
High Cademan	197m / 646 ft	56
Knoll Hill	222m / 728 ft	56
Timberwood Hill	248m / 814 ft	58
Hoton Hills	77m / 242 ft	59

Opposite, Looking towards Timberwood Hill in winter sunshine.

THE HILLS OF LEICESTERSHIRE AND RUTLAND

EIGHT OTHER HILLS NOT TO BE MISSED

Ambion Hill (120m, 394ft)

O/S Landranger 140, Summit Ref SK 401001

Ambion Hill is a hill in west Leicestershire, south of the town of Market Bosworth. The hill is the site of the deserted medieval village of Anebein. For a long time, the Battle of Bosworth was thought to have taken place on Ambion Hill. Recent research has indicated, however, that the battle probably took place to the south west near Fenn Lanes. Ambion Hill was Richard the Third's camp on the night of the battle, and now the Bosworth Battlefield Heritage Centre is situated there.

Ambion Hill lies twelve miles west of Leicester. The cortege carrying Richard the Third's remains visited the hill during the procession, before their interment in Leicester Cathedral in 2015.

The summit is a short walk from the car park at the Bosworth Battlefield Visitor Centre. There is a circular hedged enclosure at the summit with chairs for Henry V, Richard III and Lord Stanley, a good place to sit down and reflect for a few minutes.

Summit of Ambion Hill, Lord Stanley's chair on the right.

Belvoir Castle (138m, 453ft)

O/S Landranger 130, Summit Ref SK 820338

Belvoir Castle stands on the top of a hill in north east Leicestershire close to the border with Lincolnshire. It is one of the most popular places in Leicestershire. There is a charge to enter the castle gardens, and thus climb to the high point. It is a short but fairly steep walk to the high point, which is near the Mausoleum, and there are plenty of walks and gardens to explore within the grounds.

Belvoir Castle was originally a Norman Castle destroyed in 1464. The current building dates back to 1668. It has been the home of the Manners family and the seat of the Dukes of Rutland since 1703. The gardens were designed and landscaped by Elizabeth Howard, the 5th Duchess of Rutland. A corner of the castle is still used as the family home of the Manners family.

The castle is used in a number of films and television programmes including the Da Vinci code, The Young Victoria, and The Crown.

Belvoir Castle from the Rose Garden.

EIGHT OTHER HILLS NOT TO BE MISSED

Launde Park Hill (191m, 627ft)

O/S Landranger 141, Summit Ref SK 808032

Smith Hill (172m, 564ft)

O/S Landranger 141, Summit Ref SK 797053

These hills lie near Launde Abbey. I have named the lower hill, Smith Hill for convenience as it is unnamed on the map. The walk over Launde Park Hill and Smith Hill, is an excellent circular walk of around 10km (6 miles), partly on the Leicestershire Round. Launde Abbey, where I suggest starting and finishing the walk, is a large Tudor House situated in the bowl of the hills. It was built for Thomas Cromwell on the site of a wealthy priory. Cromwell only had possession for three years before his execution in 1540.

Launde Abbey.

Park at Launde Abbey and follow the Leicestershire Round north to a footbridge over the River Chater, then continue on the footpath to the top of Smith Hill (grid reference SK 797053).

Descend Smith Hill towards a barn near Withcote Hall, then turn right to walk south east then east past Avenue Farm and Cottage Farm on a Right of Way.

After passing the entrance to Withcote Lodge, the track turns into a path. Continue for another 500m to a t-junction of the paths next to some trees, turn right and walk 400m south west (staying left of the burn) to join the Leicestershire Round as it makes its way from Launde Abbey to Belton-in-Rutland. Turn left to follow the Leicestershire Round east.

View towards 'Smith Hill' from Launde Abbey.

Follow the path east to an excellent track, then turn right to follow this track south. After 1.5km the high point of the track is reached. Instead of continuing down the hill to Belton-in-Rutland, turn right to walk 100m to the Trig Point, which is in the hedge on the left, the summit of Launde Park Hill.

Continue straight over the field past Launde Park Wood and take the right-hand path at a fork, to reach the minor road from Loddington to Launde Abbey at Pt 179m. Turn right and follow the minor road down the hill to Launde Abbey. Hopefully the tea room will be open for refreshments.

EIGHT OTHER HILLS NOT TO BE MISSED

High Cademan, Whitwick (197m, 646ft)

O/S Landranger 129, Summit Ref SK 441169

The next three hills in this section lie in Charnwood Forest. High Cademan lies just north of Whitwick in a wood popular with the local residents. There is also some rock climbing in the area. The summit Trig Point is a short walk of 200m from the car park to the east. Park in the car park (grid ref SK 443168).

Summit Trig Point on High Cademan, Whitwick.

Knoll Hill, Markfield (222m, 728ft)

O/S Landranger 129, Summit Ref SK 486102

The quarry on Knoll Hill near Markfield, known as Hill Hole Quarry, was opened by Breedon Everard in 1852. The granite paving blocks and other stone products went to towns and cities all over England. The Trig Point can be reached by following a path which starts south of the car park (grid ref SK 485104). The highest point lies just north west of the Trig Point but requires a scramble to reach it.

Opposite, Picture taken from the Trig Point, showing the high point of Knoll Hill. The scramble required to reach it follows the ridge, take care if you attempt this.

EIGHT OTHER HILLS NOT TO BE MISSED

Timberwood Hill (248m, 814ft)

O/S Landranger 129, Summit Ref SK 471148

Timberwood Hill, which lies in the highest part of Leicestershire, between Bardon Hill and Birch Hill (see pages 12 & 13), is a hidden gem. Its summit area is on access land, amongst bracken and similar terrain to Bradgate Park. There is a concessionary path directly to the summit cairn from the east.

Summit of Timberwood Hill.

The best place to start the walk is from a parking area just off Warren Hills Road, a few hundred metres north west of Birch Hill Farm (grid reference SK 473137). Cross the road and walk just east of north up a good tarmac track, then go through a gate. After walking for 800m, keep left at a fork in the path and continue north on the path for another 500m. As soon as the wood is reached, a concessionary path goes off to the left. Follow this through the wood and ascend the bracken covered access land. The cairn is near a tree.

THE HILLS OF LEICESTERSHIRE AND RUTLAND

Hoton Hills (77m, 242ft)

O/S Landranger 129, Summit Ref SK 562228

Hoton Hills lies on the Cross Britain Way. This is a well signposted hiking trail of 280 miles (450km) running from Boston on the east coast of England to Barmouth on the Welsh coast. It was launched in September 2014 as part of a group of paths to raise funds for Macmillan Cancer Support.

Near the summit of Hoton Hills on the Cross Britain Way.

Hoton Hills can be climbed from just north of Hoton (grid ref SK 573228). Follow the track north west for 400m to join the Cross Britain Way, then go west and south west along the summit ridge to the high point at 77m. To the north, Stanford Hall in Nottinghamshire can be seen. This was built in the 18th Century and is now a defence and national rehabilitation centre.

The walk can be extended south west to Stanford Lane, then south to Cotes. From Cotes, the return journey goes east over Mere Hill to Prestwold, before turning north to return to Hoton.

Cycling the Hills

One of the best ways of visiting the hills of Leicestershire and Rutland is by bike. A hybrid bike is best as this allows off road cycling closer to the summits. There are quiet roads to cycle on, particularly around Charnwood Forest and East Leicestershire where many of the hills are located. A bike also eliminates any difficulty of finding a place to park near a hill. There are many routes to cycle round the hills and I have outlined four of them below.

1. The Charnwood Forest 'seven'

(22km, 14miles cycling from Bradgate Park, excludes hill walks/cycles)

Possible start points for this cycle include the Hunts Hill car park at Bradgate Park or the high car park at Beacon Hill. The cycle ride could also be started at Leicester or Loughborough but this will add about twenty miles to the total distance.

If starting at the Hunts Hill car park at Bradgate Park, it is an easy walk to Old John Tower. Now take the minor road which goes north west from the car park. After one kilometre you will reach the log gate to the east of Benscliffe Hill and Wood (see page 15).

Continue north west for 1.5km, then turn right along the B591 to the car park under Beacon Hill. A bike can be taken most of the way to the summit. Return to the B591 and cycle back to the crossroads, this time continuing on the B591 for a short distance. Turn right at grid ref SK 502141 and cycle one kilometre to the start point for Bawdon Castle Hill. The route up is described on page 16.

Continue on the minor road towards Shepshed. After 3km, the Ives Head parking area (grid ref SK 472169) is reached. Continue north up the hill to the stile then climb Ives Head (page 19). Cycle back down the hill then uphill in a south westerly direction passing Oaks in Charnwood (perhaps making a short detour to St Joseph's tea room, open Thursday to Sunday). After 2.5km, you will come to a crossroads. Go straight across and past a school. After passing the school, turn left at a sign for Bardon Hill.

THE HILLS OF LEICESTERSHIRE AND RUTLAND

Cycling up Bardon Hill.

Continue through housing estates to reach Vercor Close and the start point for Bardon Hill. After cycling or walking up Bardon Hill, return to Vercor Close and turn right out of the estate to reach the B587. The B587 passes Birch Hill where there are access problems, but it is possible to walk to the wall, see page 13. Continue to Copt Oak, and turn left then right following signs to Newton Linford. The route passes quiet country roads back to the start.

2.   **Melton Mowbray four hills circuit**

(30km, 19miles cycling, excludes hill walks)

Starting at Melton Mowbray, cycle 10km along the A606 towards Oakham. You will see a minor road going off south signposted to Cold Overton. After 1km, leave the bike at a right of way sign to climb Ranksborough Hill (see page 46). After climbing this hill continue south to Cold Overton. A short detour will enable a visit to Cold Overton Hill.

Cycle west to Somerby and then north west to Burrough Hill Country Park. The Trig Point is an easy walk. Return to the bike and go north to Gartree Hill.

Cycling the Hills (cont)

Cycle over Gartree Hill (see page 43). After 2km another minor road is reached. Continue north past the Trig Point at 122m spot height. It is a further two kilometres back to the centre of Melton Mowbray.

3. Eight hills in East Leicestershire

(45km, 28miles cycling, excludes hill walks)

From the centre of Leicester, cycle 9km to Houghton on the Hill following the A47. After Houghton on the Hill there is a constant stream of hills to climb. Cycle a further 2km east on the A47, then turn left following signposts to Tilton on the Hill on a minor road. After 3km Life Hill is reached, near a tall radio mast. Continue to Tilton on the Hill, then take the road east towards Oakham.

After one kilometre, Tilton Cutting appears, and the right of way up Colborough Hill (page 38). After this ascent, it is a short 500m cycle to Whatborough Hill. After climbing this hill, follow the road which goes off to the right at the junction below Whatborough Hill (page 36). Cycle 1.5km past a farm and the right of way skirting Robin-a-Tiptoe Hill (page 37). The cycling is now on minor roads with very few cars.

Continue east and turn right at the next junction. Cycle 1km south to a crossroads. Turn left and after 400m the path to Launde Hill is reached (see page 41). After this walk, return to the crossroads and follow the road towards Tugby. After 500m the gate next to Round Hill is passed (page 42).

From here, follow the narrow road 2.5km south east to Tugby. Café Ventoux (picture opposite) is an excellent place to stop for refreshments. Cycle south from Tugby. After one kilometre go straight across the junction with the A47, past Keythorpe Farm and up Bassett's Hill (page 28). Return to the crossroads 1km south of Tugby and turn right along Crackbottle Road to Moor Hill.

From Moor Hill, follow the road south then east to return to the crossroads 1km south of Tugby. The return to Leicester can be made on quiet roads past Illston on the Hill.

THE HILLS OF LEICESTERSHIRE AND RUTLAND

Café Ventoux at Tugby, named after a Tour de France mountain stage.

4. A round of Rutland Water and Hambleton Hill

(32km, 20miles cycling, with visit to Hambleton Hill)

The most popular cycle in Leicestershire and Rutland is the round of Rutland Water. It is a long walk, 27km (17 miles) even without Hambleton peninsula, so a popular way of circling Rutland Water is to cycle.

A good place to start is the car park at Edith Weston, near Normanton Church, where bikes can be hired. The route goes east and traverses the top of the dam on the east side of reservoir. It then heads west on cycle and walking tracks staying close to the side of the Rutland Water. Whitwell and Barnsdale are passed, then cycle along the A606 to the west end of Rutland Water. At Hambleton Peninsula there is a choice, either the longer route including the peninsula, or 5km extra to Hambleton Village to bag Hambleton Hill. Finally, head south past Egleton and east to Edith Weston.

My ten favourite hills

I have listed my ten favourite hills below with brief reasons as to why the hill is included. They are in alphabetical order

1   **Bardon Hill.** A remarkable summit with the quarry on the south side and woodland to the north.

2   **Beacon Hill.** The walk from the lower car park gives an interesting circular walk, and this is a superb summit with great views.

3   **Breedon on the Hill.** Easily identified by the spectacular cliff wall when approached from the east. The short walk up the footpath from the village to the ancient church at the summit should not be missed.

4   **Burrough Hill.** The walk up the hill from the north through a sea of yellow gorse is the best way to approach this hill in spring and early summer. On the summit you can feel the history that has passed through this old Iron Age Hill Fort.

5   **Colborough Hill.** A great little hill rising to a rounded grassy summit. There is also the chance to explore the historic Tilton Cutting next to the hill.

6   **Croft Hill.** A surprising hill rising up sharply just south of Leicester with a quarry on the east side. The western slopes have been popular with day trippers since Victorian times.

7   **Ives Head.** Shepshed's own hill with its prominent rocky summit.

8   **Langton Caudle.** A fine hill with good paths that approach the summit from both north and south. There is also a good walk around the villages and over the summit.

9   **Old John Tower.** A chance to explore historic and beautiful Bradgate Park, the birthplace of Lady Jane Grey, and see the remarkable folly, Old John Tower, at the summit.

10   **Ambion Hill.** For a long time, this was thought to be the site of the Battle of Bosworth. If you walk to the circular hedge on the summit on a summer evening you can imagine the battle over 500 years ago.

Opposite, Summit of Burrough Hill.

LISTING AND MAP OF HILLS

	TuMPS	Height		Drop	Date Climbed
1	Bardon Hill	280m	918 ft	172m	
2	Birch Hill	254m	833 ft	31m	
3	Beacon Hill	248m	814 ft	62m	
4	Benscliffe Hill	237m	778 ft	39m	
5	Bawdon Castle	232m	761 ft	34m	
6	Whatborough Hill	230m	755 ft	108m	
7	Life Hill	226m	741 ft	46m	
8	Robin-a-Tiptoe Hill	222m	728 ft	43m	
9	Colborough Hill	220m	722 ft	36m	
10	Old John Tower	212m	696 ft	35m	
11	Cold Overton Hill	211m	692 ft	44m	
12	Burrough Hill	210m	689 ft	31m	
13	Launde Hill	202m	663 ft	39m	
14	Ives Head	201m	659 ft	43m	
15	Round Hill	193m	633 ft	31m	
16	Ranksborough Hill	191m	627 ft	41m	
17	Bassett's Hill	182m	596 ft	33m	
18	Waltham/Wolds Hill	177m	581 ft	35m	
19	Mowsley Hills	177m	581 ft	66m	
20	Broughton Hill	173m	568 ft	37m	
21	Moor Hill	172m	565 ft	34m	
22	Buckminster Hill	158m	518 ft	35m	
23	Gartree Hill	148m	486 ft	36m	
24	Langton Caudle	147m	482 ft	50m	
25	South Hill	132m	433 ft	39m	
26	Slawston Hill	131m	430 ft	37m	
27	Croft Hill	128m	420 ft	44m	
28	Breedon Hill	126m	414 ft	30m	
29	Hambleton Hill	126m	413 ft	40m	
30	Wellsborough Hill	120m	394 ft	31m	
31	Prestley Hill	117m	384 ft	38m	

THE HILLS OF LEICESTERSHIRE AND RUTLAND

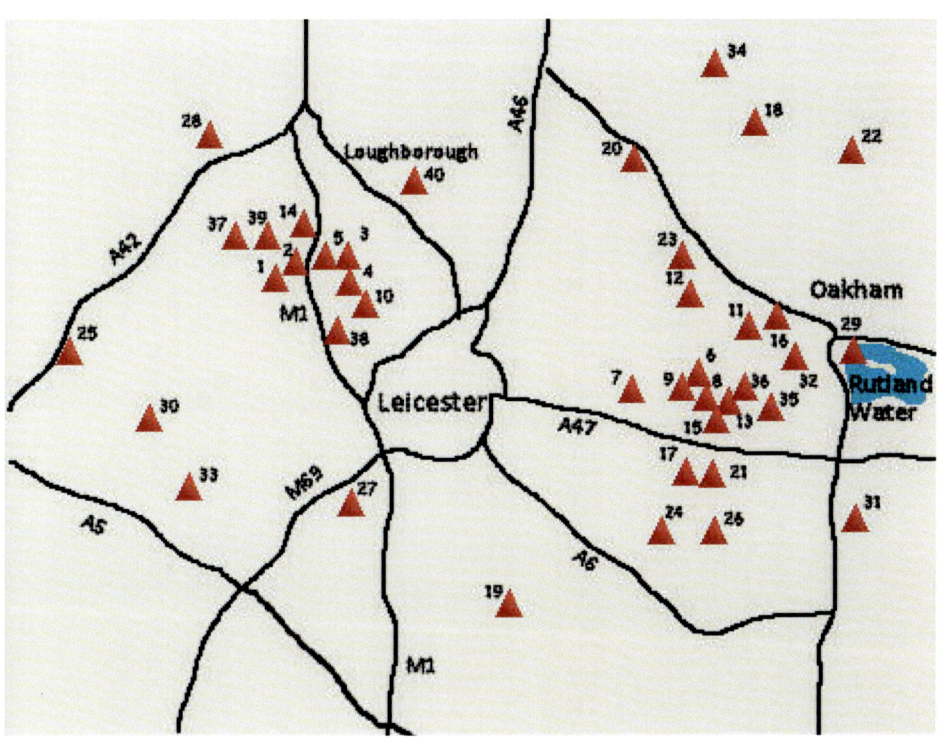

	Other Hills	Height		Date Climbed
32	Cold Overton Park Hill	197m	646 ft	
33	Ambion Hill	120m	394 ft	
34	Belvoir Castle	138m	453 ft	
35	Launde Park Hill	191m	627 ft	
36	Smith Hill	172m	564 ft	
37	High Cademan	197m	646 ft	
38	Knoll Hill	222m	728 ft	
39	Timberwood Hill	248m	814 ft	
40	Hoton Hills	77m	242 ft	

THE HILLS OF LEICESTERSHIRE AND RUTLAND

	Page No
Ambion Hill	52
Bardon Hill	11,12,13,61,64
Bassett's Hill	28
Bawdon Castle	16
Beacon Hill	14,15.64
Belvoir Castle	53
Benscliffe Hill	15
Birch Hill	13
Bosworth Battlefield	52
Bradgate Park	17,18
Breedon Hill	21,25,64
Broughton Hill	23
Buckminster Hill	24
Burrough Hill	40,64,65
Charnwood Forest	10,60
Colborough Hill	38,64
Cold Overton Hill	39
Cold Overton Park Hill	49
Croft Hill	32,64
Gartree Hill	43
Hambleton Hill	47
High Cademan	56
Hoton Hills	59
Ives Head	19,64
Keythorpe Hall Farm	28
Knoll Hill	56,57
Langton Caudle	27,30,64
Launde Abbey	41,54
Launde Hill	41

	Page No
Launde Park Hill	54
Launde Big Wood	8,41
Leicestershire Round	5
Life Hill	7,39
Lyddington Bede House	48
Moor Hill	28
Mowsley Hills	29
Normanton Church	45
Old John Tower	5,17,18,64
Prestley Hill	48
Ranksborough Hill	46
Relative Hills Society	8
Robin-a-Tiptoe Hill	37
Round Hill	42
Rutland Water	44,45,63
Slawston Hill	31
Slawston Bridge	31
Smith Hill	54
South Hill	33
Tilton Cutting	38
Timberwood Hill	58
Tugby	28,63
TuMPs definition	8
Twycross Zoo	26
Ventoux Cafe	63
Waltham-on-the-Wolds Hill	22
Wellsborough Hill	33
Whatborough Hill	35,36